THE LIGHTHOUSE

GUERNICA WORLD EDITIONS 14

THE LIGHTHOUSE

Elizabeth D. Macaluso

GUERNICA
World
EDITIONS

TORONTO—BUFFALO—LANCASTER (U.K.)
2019

Michael Mirolla, editor
Cover design: Allen Jomoc, Jr.
Interior layout: Jill Ronsley, suneditwrite.com
Front cover image: Anton Sokolov | Dreamstime.com
Guernica Editions Inc.
1569 Heritage Way, Oakville, (ON), Canada L6M 2Z7
2250 Military Road, Tonawanda, N.Y. 14150-6000 U.S.A.
www.guernicaeditions.com

Distributors:
University of Toronto Press Distribution,
5201 Dufferin Street, Toronto (ON), Canada M3H 5T8
Gazelle Book Services, White Cross Mills
High Town, Lancaster LA1 4XS U.K.

First edition.
Printed in Canada.

Legal Deposit—First Quarter
Library of Congress Catalog Card Number: 2018966971
Library and Archives Canada Cataloguing in Publication
Title: The Lighthouse / Elizabeth D. Macaluso.
Names: Macaluso, Elizabeth D., author.
Series: Guernica world editions ; 14.
Description: Series statement: Guernica world editions ; 14 | Poems.
Identifiers: Canadiana 20190043946 | ISBN 9781771833851 (softcover)
Classification: LCC PS3613.A33 L54 2019 | DDC 811/.6—dc23

To my family, friends, and colleagues,
you have made this book possible
and I am forever in your debt.

Contents

Nirvana

I see it in Sweden's fields of yellow flowers,
in Scotland's lochs that reflect mountains.
I see it in the windows of candy shops in Wales,
in the old farmhouses of New York,
and the fall foliage of Ohio. I see it
in the deserts of Arizona and the canyons of Nevada.
I see it in my love's face, in the way his eyes light up
when he laughs or smiles. His eyes are what I imagine
the firmament is, a subject that is in Mozart's music
and Angelou's poems. Elusive but ever present.

For Keziah and Joshua

My nephew, Keziah, is three.
He loves to talk with God whom he imagines is female.
"Where is she?"
He calls after God as he looks for her in the cemetery.
Keziah imagines that God is with dead people who are grumpy
because they have been buried. Still, Keziah searches for God
hoping to find her to ask her about life and death
and why people are buried, why they are grumpy
and why he cannot see her since they talk so often.
Keziah has not yet found God in all things.
He chases God as though she is in the wind,
or a wave at the beach, or inside the cracks in doors,
mausoleums, and gravestones. He insists
she is in those places even as he cannot see her.
I wonder if she is really there. But, I tell Keziah that she is.
I see her when Keziah hugs his brother, Joshua, and Joshua smiles.
I say: "Look, Keziah, look at Joshi, he's smiling!"
Surely, there is God in that.

The Lilith Fair

I took my friends to a women's concert at Jones Beach when I was sixteen.
I was so excited to see Sheryl Crow and Sarah McLaughlan,
I could hardly stand it. The music lifted me up through the clouds
and into the infinite universe.
I know that my friends were partly ashamed to be caught
at an all-girls' venue. But, they sat through it because
I wasn't ashamed and they loved me.
I still remember the love I felt for the women on stage
and the ones sitting next to me. I remember thinking
that this was what real love felt like.

Piano Man

In high school, I hated Billy Joel's songs.
I thought that they were unimaginative and boring.
I was going places. And, Billy Joel and Long Island would be left behind.
Now, when his songs come on the radio,
I am transported back to a time and place.
I remember countless barbeques in backyards
with beer, no parents, and no rules.
I remember bars with no closing times
and the same group of friends that met to talk about life.
Billy Joel is always playing in these memories.
And, I cannot escape them. They are a part of me.
They make me feel like Jack Kerouac
at Napper Tandy's or the Piano Man himself.
I think about how right he was to set it all to music.
I long for my friends and the ballads that bring us back home.

Francesca

A little girl hangs out of a car window in Brooklyn.
She's blond and ambitious;
she will wink if you pass her by.
She married this winter.
Her dress was made of feathers;
her bouquet boasted pink roses.
I will never have pink at my wedding.
It's not the right color
for a girl who likes to play with boys—
not marry them.
I often think of who I am
in relation to Francesca.
The outcome is always bleak.
I am not confident; in fact, I'm quite shy.
I will never do the things that real girls do,
like shop, and talk, and drink.
I will never hang out of a car window
without restraint, without embarrassment,
although, I wish I could.
No, I am the one inside the car,
the one who steams her breath onto the window,
whose fingers press a pattern
as they aim to get out,
to remove that glass
between herself and the world.

Nonno

You died before I was born.
But, your story lives on in my memory.
When Mussolini's men forced you to join the Italian army
you went to Africa, but, you did not fight.
You kept your family safe and stood up to a dictator.
You were captured by the British; they barely gave you food or water.
You were ill when you were released and sent back home.
You endured painful surgery and died from complications
    to that operation.
But, you live on in Nonna's words about you
and the picture that she keeps on her bedside table
next to rose petals and a rosary.
Nonna says that you were a good man.
I see you in my father and uncle.
I see your kindness, your gentleness, your good humor, and your love.
These are the ways I know you, Nonno.
These are the ways that you are alive.

Randy

You are the maintenance man for my apartment complex.
But, you keep watch over me like a father.
When I ask you: "How are you Randy?"
And, you say: "Not bad for a fat, old guy,"
I wish I could tell you that I don't see a fat, old guy.
I see a man who cares about others,
whose blue eyes sparkle,
who lives every day wishing to do his best for his family,
his work, and himself. When you say:
"I'm just a farm boy," I wish I could tell you,
in you, Randy, I see someone who insists on making life go right.
And, I thank you for making it go right for me.

Binghamton

I love your old storefronts and the people that make them come alive.
I love your breweries, pubs, and small restaurants
    from around the world.
I love your farms and farm boys.
I love your apples, raspberries, blueberries,
and the rough but gentle hands that pick them.
I love those strains of blues music that blare out of the bars.
I love your mountains, rivers, streams, and your minnows in tiny ponds.
I love your people who sparkle with possibility.
I love your frogs, deer, sheep, and cows.
I love your sunsets and sunrises.
I love your tractors and endless meadows.
I love your character and the way you feel.
I love the way you hope, create, and dream, when no one expects you to.
I love the way you rise, ever so slowly, toward the boundless sky.

Thunderstorms

My mother loved to take my sister, Catherine, and I out in them.
I remember parking at the Walt Whitman mall
and stepping out of our Volvo station wagon into a foot of water.
Mom said: "We're going to have fun, now, run!"
I ran toward the mall in the rain feeling exhilarated.
This must be what Whitman meant when he said:
"I am large, I contain multitudes!"
Emily Dickinson saw possibility in everything.
I see it in sheets of rain, light against dark,
and clouds that are thick, heavy, and wet.

Uncle Johnny's Star Trek Room

My Uncle John has a special room in his house
for his *Star Trek* memorabilia.
He showed it to me for the first time at Thanksgiving.
He told me how he coveted the talking Captain Kirks
and hand-painted replicas of Spock's enemies.
He walked me through almost every collectible he owns.
To him, they are symbols of his own sense of possibility,
his value of truth, science, and innovation.
Uncle John worked at the MTA for thirty years.
He never set foot inside of a college classroom.
He never got to discuss relativity or particle physics,
or what truth meant to Sophocles, Aristotle, or Buber.
Instead, he punched in and out of a time clock
and dotted I's and T's with his coworkers.
But, he still got to come home
and work on his *Star Trek* models and dream
of other galaxies, new dimensions, and the far reaches of space.
My cousins, Jennifer and Jonathan, are Uncle John's greatest achievements.
As he walked me through his creations, I realized that we are his future.
We are realizing his dreams with our Ph.D.'s in literature,
our professions in what we love, our work
in literature, computer science, and social work.
We live the possibility that Uncle Johnny dreams of.
His room, full of homage to *Star Trek*, is also a shrine
where he thanks some sort of God for all of our good fortune.

Love

The boy on my couch is in love with my roommate.
Night after night, he looks for her.
She pretends he isn't there.
He's always on that couch.
He lies there without any shoes on, with a blanket over him,
with the TV on, while he snores softly.
She is in the other room with the door closed.
I think about what it is like to feel like him.
It's like driving alongside a breath-taking meadow
with yellow flowers. I want to reach out and touch them
but I can't. The glass is always there;
it reminds me about my world and that of the meadow's.
It reminds me of the impermanence of the flowers
and the hardness of the glass.

The Lighthouse

My friends and I used to run towards its red and white lights.
They looked like falling stars.
We didn't know why, Eulalia, our best friend,
insisted that we stay up late to watch, and play around, these lights.
Eulalia's Coast Guard father constantly barked orders
    to his wife and daughters.
I used to wonder if they ever got tired of his routine
or the small house that they lived in
that was next to even smaller houses.
The coast guard community often felt like a prison
with people living on top of one another like sardines in a can.
But after dark, the lighthouse lights were on
and they glowed like beacons.
We took Eulalia outside, past her father's bedtime,
and ran to the sand by the shore
and shouted at the top of our lungs.
We swung on the swings
and played on the playground until dawn.
We made sure that Eulalia had a life
outside of orders. We were fashioning our dreams,
according to the stars in the sky,
and the lighthouse lights that beamed with possibility.

Zio Giorgio

He walked with me up a hill in Sicily.
He drove, in a tiny car, through meadows and mountains.
He loved his wife.
When she died, his soul died, too.
He could not help himself.
Why? I say, did he have to die this way—
amidst strangers and machines?
Did he know his family?
Did he remember me?
I don't know.
I probably never will.
But, I remember oranges,
his sweet smile, no English,
and a soul that will travel with me forever.

My Nonna Only Went to the Fifth Grade

But, she tells stories with mastery.
Her favorite story is the one about
      Uncle Pino.
Picture a modest house in the orange groves
      of Sicily.
Nonna and her six siblings sit down at the
      dinner table.
Great Grandma Pauline sits at one end. Her
      Father is to her left,
and there is an empty chair for Great
      Grandpa to her right.
They wait. Finally, Great Grandpa comes
      home,
sits down and says, *silenziu*. Nobody moves.
They wait for Great Grandpa to eat his food
so that they can eat as well. Suddenly,
out of nowhere, Uncle Pino says
Lu papa piscia! The pope pees!
Everyone erupts with laughter including
Great Grandpa.
They eat with pleasure.

After Aunt Katy passed away,
and then, Aunt Rosie, Uncle Sal, and Uncle
    Jack,
Nonna takes special pride in telling this story.
It takes her back to a time when laughter and
    joy
were as precious as the gold around her neck,
when family was everything,
when death was not a frequent houseguest,
when love radiated around a table filled with
    bread and wine,
and when hope intervened to dull the reality
    of poverty
that crept like a beggar outside their kitchen
    door.

The Wedding

Memories of my cousin's wedding will stay with me forever
like the golden sun that wrapped Joe and Michelle
    in an other-worldly light.
I will forget about the champagne in flutes
with solitary blueberries floating at their tops.
I will forget about the gifts and how many people attended the event.
I will forget about the food and dessert.
What I will remember is my ninety three-year-old Nonna
dancing to music that she will never understand
and twirling me around the dance floor
with all of our relatives and friends looking on with wonder and delight.
This memory reminds me of the love that knits our family together
like Nonna's crocheted socks and blankets.
This love is infinite and it spans generations and time.
It is a constant in a world of violent variables.
It makes me relive those moments when my sister, Catherine, and I
walked up and down Hillside Avenue in Queens, NY
to buy ice cream and rent videos with Nonna.
It makes me remember my cousins and how we grew up together.
It makes me treasure Michelle and Joe's love
and it assures me that this love will find me in my future.
This love is like the birth of a new child;
it is wondrous, unconditional, devoted, and permanent.

The Robins in Vestal, NY

The robins stand so proudly in the lush green grass.
Their fiery red breasts peek out of my neighbors' lawns
as though they are the subjects of an abstract painting,
a cubist's or a pointillist's orange dream.
Sometimes, the robins are afraid.
They don't know what to make of me as I invade their territory.
At other times, they trust me and are quiet, docile, and peaceful.
To be a robin must be dangerous and philosophical;
one must always watch out for cars, predators, and sadistic humans
who like to torture you with a rock or a stick.
And yet, the art of just sitting in the grass and seeing life
for what it truly is—a series of moments—must be satisfying,
particularly, as one catches the occasional worm.

The Garden

My sister and I played in it for hours.
We loved the stone paths that led us to grapes,
zucchini, tomatoes, basil, and fennel.
Nonna hung clothes on the line.
The scent of flowers wafted in the breeze.
My sister and I chased the smell
as though it was the iridescent light
of lightning bugs that were out after dark.
My sister and I are grown now;
we have no more time for play.
But we have framed a picture of my sister, Catherine,
at two years old, standing next to a pot of red geraniums.
The silk of their petals is crushed in Catherine's stubby fingers
as though she would like to imprint their essence on her skin,
and discover their secrets, the red of their color,
the earthiness of the potting soil, and my sister's wonder
at something that could be made so perfectly.

The Court in Vestal, New York

I know why I like to walk along the court in Vestal.
The Japanese maples are in full bloom.
The leaves stretch like hands pulsating with red and purple sap.
The wind is a constant companion.
The church is a solemn reminder.
But the houses are closed
as if no one wants to be in the natural world anymore.
We've decided that the virtual world is better,
with its computerized gun battles
that now take place in our streets, movie theaters, and schools.
Tonight, as I went for my walk,
I saw an elderly couple sitting on their porch.
They held hands; they were just sitting and enjoying the rain
as if all that mattered to them was their love and the earth.

For Becky

We met in third grade on the jungle gym.
You were tall, thin, blue-eyed, and lovely.
We chased each other around the playground.
We laughed, held hands, had secrets, and played
until the sun went down. I still remember
the orange and gold of that sun as it sunk below the horizon,
as if our childhood, too, was disappearing, its innocence ending.
I remember the first time I slept at your house.
Your mother woke us up in the middle of the night
to find money for drugs. Her voice was harsh,
cruel, and desperate. You were so embarrassed.
Later that night, you woke me up, held my hand
and told me how your father used to beat your mother.
It was the first time I had ever heard of such brutality,
such violence in the home. I held your hand as you cried.
I didn't know what else to do.
I clutched your hand as if our embrace had magical powers,
as if it would take us back to my house where there was love.
You would be safe there.
You would never have to worry about being hit,
or neglected, or humiliated. I thought
that you could be a part of our family
even as another part of me knew that this was an impossibility.
Eventually, we grew apart. You came to my sweet sixteen.

I never saw you after that. But, I imagine that you are safe and happy
with a family of your own. I hope that this fantasy is true,
even as I know that it may not be.
You might be running around Long Island
drunk, or too high to know yourself.
But, I still remember that girl on the playground
and how kind, honest, and sweet she was.
I hope that you are still her.

Remembering Vincenzina

The first time I saw my father cry,
he struggled to remember her name.
He knew her by her half-curved smile
and the suffering that seeped through salt-water eyes.
He told my mother: "This is my neighbor, Vincenzina Petrolia."
I looked at her.
She was very old and very small.
Her bones were as brittle as a baby bird's.
Her face was like a stone.
It bore the collective fortitude of those who stayed behind
while others had to leave and sigh …

The tears my father shed for Vincenzina
beside an orange grove *in Sicilia*
told me that she was his mother
when there was no one else,
when they all left, *dopo la guerra*.
She remained.
She stood on the edge of the mountain.
She cried for a lost little boy
who climbed over the mountain
to meet people she did not know.

Grief

It troubles me that there are people in the world who suffer,
like the girl who lets her boyfriend repeatedly rape her;
like the man who owns the pizza shop
who'll never make enough money
to attract the woman he'd like to marry;
like the mother whose son was killed in a crash
on Route 61 more than twenty years ago;
like the drug addict, the boozer, the lifelong patient of plastic surgery,
the men who call themselves "the enlightened ones."
It troubles me that there are people like this.
Even if I stood at their doors and begged them to come back to life,
they'd never hear me. Still, I'd stand there—shouting!

Grandma

I thought that I hated you.
You, with your dark and dreary house,
your phone that barely works, your half-cooked ham at Christmas.
You, with your costume jewelry, your cracked lip-stick,
your clothes that barely fit, and your children's bedrooms
    that will never change.
But, you always brought chewing gum for long trips.
You always remember my birthday with a card or a gift.
You call me "teacher of the year."
You love me, even as you cannot love yourself.

For My Friends

We met in kindergarten and painted
brightly colored hands on our classroom wall.
We called our boyfriends from plastic telephones
and always called them "Bobby."
We had our first sleepovers together.
On Halloween, we went trick-or-treating in Eaton's Neck
and collected candy bars, gum, and games.
We sat together at school.
We had wonderful parties.
We made each other mixed tapes of all of our favorite songs.
But, we also got each other through abuse,
alcoholism, drugs, imperfect parents,
classroom rivalries, heartbreaks, and separations.
We never told each other that we loved each other.
But, we knew it. Our matching tattoos attest to this.
And, we take this love to our graves.
It is what brought us to college, to success,
to our lives, our loves, our families, our new friends.
Even, now, as I write this poem, I hear Dianna's voice
telling me that I am good at something,
that I am talented, that I am worthwhile.
This, and only this, has guided my hand all of these years.
And, like our tattoos, it is always there.

When You Are a Girl from Long Island

You live for adventure.
You ride your bike into the endless woods.
You don't care when you scrape your knee.
You witness multiple sunrises because you are out until dawn.
These sunrises are blue, purple, and indigo at Crab Meadow
and peach, champagne, and goldenrod at Montauk.
You lay out at the beach until you are red with sunburn.
You don't tell your parents about countless bonfires
in nameless backyards where you'll find liquor,
boys, girls, and stupid fun.
You have circles of friends that last forever,
even as some relationships fade into memory.
You are still known for your shenanigans
with that same group of girls
who will never leave you, even after you move away,
and there are weddings, babies, and spouses.
You travel to the tip of the island and look across the shore.
You long for your life,
and what you will be when you leave it.

For My Husband

You noticed me at an academic talk about servitude.
I was offended by the way the critic
made Indian history a Western subject.
I raised my hand and told her
that she had mapped classical Greece onto India,
silencing the peoples and histories of that place.
I looked at my Indian friends in the room
and said: "I wonder what my colleagues would say about this?"
My friends Riya and Wakar raised their hands
and spoke back to this woman.
You sat still and looked at me.
Your eyes made me feel alive and empowered all at once.
I felt special, like I was the only critic and woman in the room.
We never spoke to each other that day.

You kept sitting next to me at talks.
I talked with you about my life,
the projects I was realizing
and the things I was making happen.
You listened and supported me.
I shared my poems with you.
Many of my poems contain a longing for a husband,
who is as good as my father, uncle, and relatives have been.
One poem tells my Zio Giorgio's story
about how much he loved his wife.
I remember how true this love was.

I associate it with the oranges
my Uncle shared with me
while he told me how much he loved her.
When I saw you share an orange with me,
after you read my poem,
I knew I found my husband at last.

Uncle Giuseppe Rumore

The mafia shot you in front of your home
because you were a socialist.
You dared to imagine the world differently
from the fascists who took your life.
Your last name means "to make noise" in Italian.
You told our relatives stories
about what it means to love one another
and to look out for the common man.
You were not afraid of the men in power.
You lived your life according to a higher truth
about a brotherhood of man.
Now, when I see my husband write about a New America,
one that includes everyone,
and values the work of the maid and the laborer,
I think of you, Uncle Giuseppe.
You imagined Italy as a strong and united nation
that was not corrupt and that looked out for its people.

If you were alive today,
I think you would be proud
of the Italian Americans,
and all Americans,
who stand up for truth
in the face of lies,
who remember that we are one nation,
under God that is indivisible,

that stands strong against violence,
even when the barrel of a loaded gun
is pointed directly at our faces,
asking us to stand down,
even when we insist on
taking that bullet in the chest
in the name of our lives,
our loves, our families,
and our freedom.

Christina

You are the only girl in a family of boys,
but you were born with a wild soul
and blue eyes that speak of brilliance.
God placed you in my arms
as a little daughter I will always look after.
But, you don't need any coddling.
You run and play and argue just like your brothers.
You play the trumpet, excel at school, and have many friends.
You have never needed your family to help you with anything,
even as you like the fact that we are there for you.
When your first boyfriend dumped you,
because you are Italian,
I wanted to sit him down and sing your praises,
and tell him how amazing you are.
In a world where men can still be cruel,
you move forward, my darling Christina,
and insist that you have
the life that you want for yourself.
Your music teaches people
that they are not alone,
that there is beauty and goodness in the world,
and that women are at its forefront.
You do all of this at seventeen.
You have lived lifetimes that many dream about.
Go confidently into the world and make it better,
with your blue eyes, blond hair, quick wit,
deep soul, loving heart, and impenetrable mind.

Aunt Rosie

You made the best pizza in the world!
You loved your husband, Uncle Joe Terranova,
and delighted in the tricks he played on the family.
When he died, you did not mourn like the women in Sicily
who wore black dresses and veils for life.
You went to Florida and found boyfriends there.
You had this infectious laugh.
I loved the way you said my name: "Lisabetta!"
You loved to share stories with Nonna
and you both giggled about your rump sizes.
You loved life, Aunt Rosie,
but you did not shy away from the pain it can hold.
When Kerry Jean was depressed,
you made her pizza.
When Nonna lost Nonno,
you held Nonna as she cried
and kept her company with stories, love, and laughter.
When you died, you left your daughters precious gifts
and you made sure the family was remembered in your will.
Aunt Rosie, I will remember what you gave me.
I will remember the hand-knitted slippers and hat that I still wear.
I will remember the love that went into making them.
They remind me of you and who you were,
a joyful, passionate, and compassionate person,
one that the world deeply misses.

Lois

You look like Carmela Soprano with your frosted hair
    and blood-red nails.
Someone might mistake you for a "typical Long Islander."
But, you coached the dance team at my high school,
so I was forced to like you.
I really had no reason to care for you.
You could be cruel and unpredictable.
You often told me to "stick my chest out,"
and to "wear makeup," or to "part my hair."
This was you on a good day.

However, my adolescent anger over you has softened and disappeared.
It helps me to remember that you probably came from a broken home.
You wanted to dance or act, professionally, and never had your chance.
Still, I will never understand why you didn't choose me to be captain
of the dance team. I worked so hard to earn that position—
    and I did earn it.

When I look back on these memories of you,
I realize that I already earned captain
and all the accolades and accomplishments
that I wanted for myself in high school.
You, Lois, made sure that Lauren Turano,
Amy Gillmor, and Coryn Shiflet
had their moments in the sun,
that they felt the same way that I did
as I succeeded in the real world.

Elizabeth D. Macaluso

You praised me when I got into Oberlin,
when not many others, besides my family and friends, did.
It is these moments of real goodness, Lois,
that I will remember about you.
Underneath all of your surfaces,
it is the authenticity that I will remember,
and miss most, about you.

Victoria's Secret

I walk past the hordes of giddy teenage girls,
the lip glosses and perfumes,
and choose a white, lacy bra,
some sexy lingerie.
I imagine how much you will like it.
You will call me beautiful,
and we will both think of Italian lace,
and the sanctity, the rightness, of our love.
Our love is a precious gift
that we share with one another
with kisses, words, and embraces.
I look at the young girls in Victoria's Secret
and pray that they will find, or wait,
for the love that I have with you.
They are so young. And, this place,
with its multi-colored bras and panties,
seems to encourage fun and not love.
I think of the way that Victoria's Secret
profits from young women's broken hearts.
I pray, again, that these women
will be able to choose a love like yours,
or simply walk by the store
unmoved by its red-light look.

Laura

We met in ninth grade; we were both on the dance team.
We didn't know, then, that we would be best friends.
You are the only one who knows what it is like,
to be Italian American, to be successful, and to be in love with a man.
When we were younger, we had separate circles of friends
but, we always made our way back to one another
to talk, play games, watch movies, and laugh.
It's the stories that we tell each other
that knit us together like sisters.
We've gotten through family members' illnesses and deaths,
medical school and doctoral work in literature and poetry,
heartbreaks and real love. I watched you get married
and you listened to me as I found real love.
Now that you are pregnant with your son,
I look forward to this new addition to our families
just as I have always looked forward to our get togethers,
our time together, like your new baby, is so precious and so loved.

Nonna

I think your life is like the roses in your backyard.
They bloom all too quickly but beautifully.
They are what I imagine your youth was like.
You were young and vibrant, a happy wife to your husband,
unblemished by life's pain or tragedy.
After Nonno died, you became like the early roses in midsummer.
Their petals are almost gone
though they are still fragrant and lovely.
I would have traveled through time
to know you in your youth.
I want to know what Nonno looked like.
I want to know all your brothers and sisters,
and the stories they told you,
and the music they played for you.
I want to watch Uncle Pino serenade Aunt Concetta.
I do not want to watch you die, Nonna,
like the early roses in your garden,
their beauty lasting for a moment.
I can only make more memories
with you. I will never forget our walks, our chats,
our food, and our favorite TV programs.
I'll never forget your stories or your neighbors,
or the way that Aunt Genie lived right around the corner.
I'll never forget you, Nonna, or the way that we danced
together at Joe and Michelle's wedding,
or the way that you called me repeatedly
when I became a doctor.

Elizabeth D. Macaluso

Even when your petals are gone, Nonna,
when you have returned to the earth,
I'll make sure that you have roses on your headstone,
so that you can be with Nonno once more.

Binghamton II

You are a complicated place.
You with your drug addicts and prostitutes,
your children who are hungry and have no curfews.
Your winters are too long and in summer your people are on the streets.
However, when the sun goes down, in late spring,
I see fathers teaching their sons to catch.
I see lovers holding hands as they walk along your paths.
I see boys playing basketball, owning your stretch of asphalt.
And, I see an old man admire the sunset
as if he is not sure that he will see it again.
These are the moments, Binghamton,
when your people come together,
even though their lives couldn't be more different.
Your sunsets draw them close.
They are wrapped in your yellow light.
You are mother to their pain
and are privy to their hopes.
This is why your summers last.
Your people need to look at
the breath-taking endlessness of your sky,
so that they can stay alive.

I Used to Believe in God

I used to believe in God, because I've seen things that I cannot explain.
After Robin Williams passed away, and I thought, "what a shame,"
I took a walk and saw a family of deer grazing on my neighbors' lawn.
These deer never appear during the day;
they only show themselves at night.
But, they were there, then,
as if they wished to comfort me,
and the world,
for such a heavy loss.

When Uncle Pino died only his immediate family was with him.
He told my cousins that he could see my grandfather, Nonno,
and Nonno was talking to him,
and saying that everything was alright.

I've anticipated things.
My dissertation, in part, explores violence against Victorian women.
My committee and I spoke about this violence.
I had a strange feeling that this violence would come again,
not to me, but, to someone else.
Two weeks later, the bombing in Manchester
against Ariana Grande happened.
I thought about how uncanny this was.
I lamented the fact that violence could be brought
    against so pure a person,
someone who only wished to bring light into the world.

These are the things that I cannot explain.
I hope they are coincidences.
I hope that they can be explained by science.
I want to know the answers.
I want to know the secrets to everyone and everything.
However, part of me still hopes
that there is a God,
even as most of me is sure that there is not.
It would be wonderful
to be connected to everyone,
to have networks of family and friends
that exist on earth and some other plain.
Then, I know that Robin Williams, Uncle Pino,
and the Manchester victims did not die in vain,
that there is meaning and purpose to it, to us
and that love really can bind us to one another
even in the face of great loss.

Elizabeth D. Macaluso

CCD (Confraternity of Christian Doctrine)

Most people do not understand Catholicism,
at least, not the Catholicism that I was taught
by my friends' mothers and Father Ryan.
When I was in the first, or second grade,
I went to the Berger's house,
and I learned about Lent, Easter, and Christmas.
We shared cookies and were close.
It felt like family; this community of friends.
We ran outside, played tag, and watched the lightning bugs
dance for us. There was no scripture, no brutalized Jesus,
no sins, no regret, no trapped feeling, no Father,
just friends and fun. I noticed that my church,
Our Lady Queen of Martyrs, was different
from the other dioceses, like St. Philip Neri's.
Father Ryan invited us into his home.
He showed us his super soaker water gun
that he used to play with his nephews and nieces.
He never made us recite scripture or confess.
He liked being with us and we liked him too.
As I grew up, religious education became about how to treat others.
This is why I have reverence for people and their stories.
In our CCD group, my friend, Michael, talked about his sister's rape
for the first time. At mass, I saw a man who really was a woman
join our prayers. To this day, I visit my church to be near the water, Mary,
and a community of like-minded people, who believe that meditation,

finding and practicing possibility, and treating others with dignity,
is essential to success.
Prayer, for me, is about what I can do in this world;
it is about sharing my songs and stories with you.

Uncle Pino

You were so quiet all the time that I knew you.
But, you could play the guitar
without any lessons and sing songs of Sicily.
Did you know that you were a poet?
The songs you sang were love songs,
about men courting and loving their wives,
with the greatest reverence, like Petrarch for Laura,
and you, Uncle Pino, for Aunt Concetta.
I think about what it must have been like to be serenaded,
to know the love that you and Aunt Concetta knew.
But I do know what this love feels like.
It is in those rare moments,
when one person stands up for another,
when they promise to love one another forever,
when children are born,
when families are made.
It's these lessons that you taught me, Uncle Pino,
even though your English was broken,
I learned what it is to love from you.

Rachel

We worked together at Barnes and Noble.
We enjoyed cataloging books and brewing coffee.
One night, you invited me to your house to have a cup of tea.
We talked and you told me about your illness, your anorexia.
My body felt a sad weight on it
like someone was sitting on my chest.
I thought to myself—How is this possible?
How could this beautiful, smart, and lovely girl have an illness like this?
You told me about your parents' divorce; it was really bitter and awful.
It must have tasted like foxglove or any herb
that is designed to poison or kill you.
You told me that you needed control and you found it in food.
I felt that weight, again, like someone was holding me underwater.

But, the weight has been lifted.
You married recently.
I saw pictures of the wedding.
You and your husband look so happy.
You triumphed over science.
You triumphed over an illness that is menacing.
And, it is gone.
You are happy and healthy.
Your parents' mistakes did not ruin you.
You stood for love in the face of great difficulty.
Look at what love has given you.

I want to share your story with the world, Rachel,
because, far too often, it is ignored.
No one should ignore recovery, health, or happiness,
or treat those things as trivial subjects.
These things are the gifts of life.
You wear them like your wedding dress so boldly.
I want people to know that their past traumas
do not define their presents or futures.
It is a privilege to live, to live life well, and to be happy.
You, Rachel, are a testament to this.
You did not give up.
You did not give in.
And, look what you have done.

Catherine

You were born with beautiful brown eyes,
curly hair, and a measureless heart.
I used to hold and look at you as if you were my baby,
my sweet and special baby.
As we grew up, we started to fight; these fights were very violent.
I think about why no one stopped us!
But we've come back to each other.
I was there for you during your first relationship.
I loved spending time with you in Brooklyn.
I loved being at your graduations.
I will never forget the way you did my hair
on the day that I became a doctor.
You looked into my eyes,
smoothed my hair, adjusted my cap and gown,
pinned a rose to my chest, and said: "You look pretty."
I said: "I love you." We hugged.
We knew that we were sisters.

To John

We used to play together when we were little.
I'll never forget the way that you sauntered onto my lawn
with your Ghostbusters proton pack on your back
and your taser in your hands.
I was sitting and admiring the grass.
We suggested that we play together.
We played almost every afternoon of our lives
from kindergarten to high school.
We played restaurant, house, Star Wars, and Legos.
One day, your friend, Steven, came to play with us.
Steven said that you liked me "like boyfriends and girlfriends do."
I was shocked. Our friendship was so pure and we felt like family,
like brother and sister. I did not want that to change.
We were ten or so; I had no idea about
what boys and girls usually did together.
So, we stayed friends. But, you never asked me to be your girlfriend.
If you had, I would have thought about it, and said: "Yes."
But, you never did. I think about that to this day.
Still, we were friends and we still are friends for life.
We went to the prom together; we stayed in touch.
You're married, now, with a family of your own.
You have a wife and two daughters.
I hope that you will always treasure our friendship,
and how we played together on the corner
of Franklin and Sun Valley courts,
and that there is a bit of me in you.

Paul

You were my first boyfriend.
We danced the Tigerette Christmas Dance together,
and, for the first time, someone noticed me.
You liked me for me, my intellect, who I was,
where I was going, and I liked you for the same reasons.
But, youth is so complicated.
My best friend, Kristen Harvey, liked you, too.
I could never betray her by being romantic with you.
I wish that I had told you this,
maybe, we could have worked it out.
But, any relationship would be ruined
if it meant the end of another friendship.
And, you never talked with me
about the exciting prospect of going to college,
and the fact that I would become a literary critic and poet.
You were very focused on yourself.
You were going to become a doctor.
I could already tell that you didn't want a partner,
an equal, you wanted a trophy wife,
someone who could pander to you and your journey.
Now that I have found a love
that caters to me and me only,
the gendered politics of our first relationship, Paul, are clear to me.
I am happy that you have a career and a wife and son.
I wonder if you ever think of me.
I'll never know, but, this poem is a testament
to youth and truths about first loves.

Cody

We met in a blues bar in Endicott, NY.
Jimi Hendrix's ghost was in your guitar that night.
You talked to me.
I knew that this talk might lead to a date.
I thought to myself: "What is this talented man
doing in a bar like this?" He should be in school
for music or performing as a studio musician.
But, poverty is an indiscriminate mistress.
When she has hold of you, she won't let go.
I wanted to save you.
I wanted to introduce you to my musician friends
and get you a job playing the tunes that you love.

But, what if you didn't want to be saved?
What if I gave my life to you and you failed me?
Isn't there a world where you and I could love each other?
Isn't there a place where money wouldn't matter?

I knew that you would ask me out.
I guided you to another topic of conversation.
It was the right thing to do—right?—
to leave now and not hurt one another.
Our conversation ended amicably.
But, I haven't gone back to the bar,
and I know that I won't visit it, again.
Sometimes, I still see you in my mind's eye.
You are playing your guitar
and it makes me smile.

Mr. Hosie

You were the only male teacher at Norwood Avenue School.
Your memory burns in my brain like a lit match.
You taught us to make ice cream with science.
We navigated our playground with compasses that led us to treasure.
We marched to physical education in lines. You skipped
and clicked your heels all the way down the hall.
Math was exciting and language was a dream.
You were brave enough to make learning fun, Mr. Hosie.
I wonder if anyone ever praised you for the good you did.
You raised intrepid and successful students.
You may have been the last of your kind.
But you skipped down to the gym
and that image will blaze in my memory forever.

Crab Meadow

The local beach, Crab Meadow, is ten minutes
   from my childhood home.
Some people, Long Islanders, define their lives around the beach.
I wouldn't say that I am one of these people.
There is more than sun and sand.
But I remember when John took me to the beach,
after we had been separated for the first time.
I was at college and he was at home in Northport.
We ran across the sand and boardwalk
like we were five years old, again.
I remember laying out at Crab Meadow
with my girlfriends for countless summers.
Ice cream, the radio, and boys were unspoken pleasures.
The beach is next to a community of Northporters.
I remember sleepover breakfasts by the shore.
I remember the way the beach is next to the marsh
where little animals make their homes.
I watched the herons, frogs, snails, and hermit crabs
all my life, as if they told me the secrets of their domain,
their home, that has been preserved to this day,
the last remnants of Long Island's marine history.
I still go back to the beach, and the marsh,
to pay tribute to this conservation
and to the memories that make me know that I am happy.

Hermit Crabs

They used to walk along the beach at Crab Meadow and Hobart Sands.
They were the last ancestors of a prehistoric race.
They looked so strange. They were like helmets
on top of little crab bodies and legs.
We were afraid of them,
which is why we turned them over on their backs
so they could not walk.
We never stopped to think that they might die.
Is this why we make war against one another?
We are afraid of each other
so we shoot to kill
until we actually do kill each other?
How many civilizations are like hermit crabs?
I used to see them walk across the beach.
Then, I saw their shells, their skeletons, litter the sand.
Now, they are gone.
There are no more shells and no more bodies.
It is as if they were never here.
I want to write a poem for the hermit crabs.
It is a bit of an apology, or an elegy,
for their brown bodies, their delicate legs, and their soft underbellies.
I imagine that we have left them alone
and they have swum out to sea
or they are just strolling along another part of the beach that I cannot see.
I wonder if they are happy,
if they are gorging themselves on minnows, or plankton, or seaweed.
That's what I would do if I were in hermit crab heaven,
with all of my hard-shelled friends.

The X-Files

The X-Files was on Fox every Sunday night, at nine,
for almost the entirety of my adolescence.
My friends and I tuned in to the show every week.
We became so involved with it that we wrote its fan fiction.
We even went scavenger hunting for X-phily themed memorabilia.
My friends loved the fact that Mulder and Scully were "a thing."
But I loved the show because it talked about truth.
Can truth be found in Scully's science or Mulder's belief?
Is it in a mixture of the two?
I loved Scully as a scientist and Mulder as a behavioral theorist.
I was mesmerized by their debates and I thought:
this is what my future will be.
And like most fans of the show,
I was intrigued by Mulder and Scully's partnership.
It was the first time that I saw an equal partnership on television.
As time went on, the show's brilliant writing faded
and the actors didn't want to be Mulder or Scully anymore.
But I still hoped that my two heroes would be together in the end.
Mulder and Scully never married
but their partnership taught me
that it is possible for two people to love one another
and to treat each other with respect.
In a subsequent television series, *Bones*,
the two heroes, Bones and Booth, do marry one another
    and have children.

In a world that makes it seem as though
you can either have a career or a marriage,
Scully and Bones had both.
They, like me, are unwilling to compromise their careers,
their passions, for anyone or anything.
We do this while making love and marriage possible.
To all of my friends and colleagues who do this,
my time with, and memories of, *The X-Files* are for us.
We should never give up on any aspect of our lives.

Krystal

People said that your family was strange
and you had nothing to recommend you.
I heard rumors that your father cheated on your mother
and that you tried to be in honors classes in school but couldn't make it.
Still, I saw that you loved life.
You were kind, fiercely loyal, and a good friend.
What does the world know about afternoons spent
making the best tomato sauce I've ever tasted?
What about those long drives on the LIE
in your convertible with the top down?
What about those moments spent at the park,
splashing around in the pool,
or watching a beloved movie?
You loved me.
You were my friend.
You were privy to my hopes and dreams.
You kept watch over these possibilities
like a hawk that guards her young.
Even as we've separated,
your memory lives in my heart and in these lines.

Ms. Uruburu's English Class

We were an intrepid group of twenty students.
I still remember all of us sitting in that bright room,
the sun shining through the windows,
and Ms. Uruburu in the front of the room.
Her classroom felt safe and secure
like one of Aunt Rosie's hugs.
My friends that I grew up with were all in the room.
We could talk about anything in that classroom.
We talked about Shakespeare and Dickens, Wharton and Chopin.
I was going to be a critic, a Victorianist and poet.
Ms. U's stories about Edith Wharton and Kate Chopin,
women who dared to be different and succeed at their crafts,
spoke to me, as if these stories told my future.
Now that I am a published Victorianist and poet,
I can say with certainty that this is due
to the lessons I learned with Ms. U.
She and I both knew that I would work hard,
write with an appreciation for the written word,
and insist on realizing my dreams.
Ms. U never judged us.
If we were female, black, Latina, Italian, gay, or troubled,
she didn't make life difficult for us.
She made it easy for us by teaching us
how to read, write, and succeed.

Oberlin

I love Tappan Square in the fall
and the way I walk along its paths amid autumn leaves.
The way to Fairchild Chapel is clear,
bringing me home to madrigals and Monteverdi.
I always found my way to Mudd Library
to read, and write, poems, my sole and secret hobby
that has turned into my profession.

Things about you, Oberlin, were not always beautiful or right.
I had an advisor who did not think I was literary because I am Italian.
I had a roommate who hated me, because I asked her
if she'd like to share my TV.
Oberlin is a solitary campus. I had to get used to being alone.

However, I went on. I survived. I moved forward.
I changed my advisor and found a group of friends who believed in me.
I played my flute for Michel Debost and sang with Steven Plank.
I studied abroad in London and lived for the theater.
I made lifelong friends in Baldwin, the Women's Collective.
And, I am close with my mentors to this day.

Amidst all of that pain and struggle and isolation, I found myself.
Now, I know why Oberlin is "a magical place"
full of Julie Taymors, Ed Helmses, Alan Menckens, and Lena Dunhams.
It is the community of people that will never let you fail,
regardless of how hard things get.

And, now, it's my turn to change the world
to give back to a solitary, little place in Ohio
that has given me so much.

Elizabeth D. Macaluso

Montauk

My friends and I pooled all of our money together
and rented a little campsite at the tip of the Island.
We stayed at the beach all day, played volleyball,
chased boys, made food, and watched innumerable sunsets.
We wanted to know that we would be friends
through college, marriage, and families.
On the last night of our week away, we stayed together in the tent.
We roasted marshmallows and told stories.
This night felt strange to me,
different from all of our other get togethers
when we knew that we would see each other
for weeks and years to come.
On the precipice of our leaving to go to college,
the silence of our sleep
felt more special to me. It felt like we were wrapped
in one of Nonna's blankets.
Our love for one another knitted us together.
No one could separate us, or break our bond,
even if we slept in our own sleeping bags
and would eventually go our own ways.
I'll never forget that night in Montauk.
It assures me that everything is possible, and attainable,
and that love, when it is true, never dies.

Acknowledgments

I would like to acknowledge Maria Gillan and the ways in which her mentorship has been vital to the success of this book. I would also like to acknowledge my colleagues from Oberlin College, St. John's University, and Binghamton University who helped to inspire and support this manuscript. I would also like to honor my friends and family. Your stories have made this volume what it is.

About the Author

Dr. Elizabeth D. Macaluso taught British literature and rhetoric and composition at Binghamton University where she received her doctoral degree. She currently works at Queensborough Community College (CUNY), where she teaches and tutors writing to undergraduate and graduate students. Liz has published her poetry in *VIA*, *Arba Sicula*, *The Paterson Literary Review*, and *The San Diego Poetry Annual*. Also, her critical book *Gender, The New Woman, and the Monster* is scheduled for publication in 2021. Liz has earned the Alfred Bendixen Award for Distinguished Teaching by a Graduate Student in English and the Graduate Student Excellence Award in Teaching as a result of her mentorship of Binghamton University undergraduates. Liz also has received numerous awards and opportunities to present her work at national and international conferences. She is always attuned to the academic job market and currently lives with her family in Northport, NY.